How to be Among the 1%

How to Join the Extremely Rich People in the World

Lloyd Wright

Text Copyright © Lloyd Wright

All rights reserved. No part of this guide may be reproduced in any form without permission in writing from the publisher except in the case of brief quotations embodied in critical articles or reviews.

Legal & Disclaimer

The information contained in this book and its contents is not designed to replace or take the place of any form of medical or professional advice; and is not meant to replace the need for independent medical, financial, legal or other professional advice or services, as may be required. The content and information in this book has been provided for educational and entertainment purposes only.

The content and information contained in this book has been compiled from sources deemed reliable, and it is accurate to the best of the Author's knowledge, information and belief. However, the Author cannot guarantee its accuracy and validity and cannot be held liable for any errors and/or omissions. Further, changes are periodically made to this book as and when needed. Where appropriate and/or necessary, you must consult a professional (including but not limited to your doctor, attorney, financial advisor or such other professional advisor) before using any of the suggested remedies, techniques, or information in this book.

Upon using the contents and information contained in this book, you agree to hold harmless the Author from and against any damages, costs, and expenses, including any legal fees potentially resulting from the application of any of the information provided by this book. This disclaimer applies to any loss, damages or injury caused by the use and application, whether directly or indirectly, of any advice or information presented, whether for breach of contract, tort, negligence, personal injury, criminal intent, or under any other cause of action.

You agree to accept all risks of using the information presented inside this book.

You agree that by continuing to read this book, where appropriate and/or necessary, you shall consult a professional (including but not limited to your doctor, attorney, or financial advisor or such other advisor as needed) before using any of the suggested remedies, techniques, or information in this book.

Table of Contents

INTRODUCTION 5

CHAPTER ONE: BE THE BOSS 7

CHAPTER TWO: KNOW YOUR MISSION 10

CHAPTER THREE: TAP THE POWER OF PROFIT 15

CHAPTER FOUR: SAVE BIG 20

CHAPTER FIVE: EARN MORE 26

CHAPTER SIX: THINK LIKE A BILLIONAIRE 33

SUMMING UP 38

About The Author 40

INTRODUCTION

For many, money is a mystery. However, for society's elite, money making is an art. It's not the numbers that are complicated – the math behind wealth-building is shockingly simple – but it's the mental baggage that bogs us down: the psychology, the emotions, the discipline, the peer pressure.

While the majority of Americans struggle with their personal finances, the elites or the 1% as I like to call them, struggle with choices of Billion dollar investments to make, yatches, super cars and luxury items to purchase, and secret vacation destinations.

I want to change that.

This guide to financial freedom has one goal: To teach you the fundamentals of financial independence.

If you implement the ideas in this book, you will build wealth. But this is no "get rich quick" scheme, these concepts are time-tested (and math-tested) methods for making and managing money. They're the very same techniques that quiet millionaires have been using for generations to accumulate cash and retire early.

CHAPTER ONE
BE THE BOSS

Here's the fundamental premise of my philosophy: You should manage your personal finances the way a business owner would manage theirs.

CALCULATING NET WORTH

My goal is to teach you how to run your life like a business. I want you to earn enormous profits so that you can use the money to do whatever it is you dream of doing. But just as I had to start at the very beginning, you will too.

Before we begin, I have a task for you. I want you to take a snapshot of your current financial position by calculating your net worth. I'll explain how.

To measure the value of a business, companies talk about equity or "book value". Jargon, right? In personal finance, equity is known as net worth. It's exactly the same thing but on a personal level.

Your net worth is an important number because it reveals how much the business of you is worth at the moment.

Still clear as mud? Maybe this definition of net worth from the blog *Wait But Why* will make more sense:

"What would happen if you sold everything you own, liquidated any investments you have, paid off all of your debts, and withdrew whatever cash

you have in bank accounts? You'd be standing on the street naked, with nowhere to go, holding a bunch of cash, and people would be looking at you. And whatever cash you were holding would be your net worth."

Net worth tracks your financial wealth in the same way that weight measures your fitness. Neither number tells the whole story, but as a measure of change over time for each is a handy tool.

Calculating net worth is easy. It's what you own minus what you owe. That's it. Simple, right? Here's how to calculate your own net worth:

1. List your assets. Check all of your bank accounts and note their balances. If you have investment and/or retirement accounts, write down how much you have in them. If you own your home, use Zillow to determine its current value. If you own a car, figure out how much it's worth. Add all of these together to find the total value of your assets.

2. Next, list your liabilities. Write down how much you owe on your car, the current balance of your mortgage, how much you have left on your student loans. Record the balance of each credit card and personal loan. The sum of everything you owe represents your total liabilities.

3. Subtract what you owe from what you own. Your net worth is your assets

minus your liabilities.

Once you've calculated your net worth, write this number down. Burn it onto your brain. I want you to remember how much you're worth today so that we can see the progress you've made in six months. And a year. And ten years. As the business of you begins to make a profit, your net worth will grow.

CHAPTER TWO
KNOW YOUR MISSION

WHAT DO YOU WANT OUT OF LIFE?

Maybe that seems like a strange question in a book about financial freedom. What has goals got to do with becoming a money boss? Everything! Having a personal mission is key to running your life like a business. Your goals help you decide how to spend your time and money.

WHAT'S YOUR WHY?

What do you want out of life?

Too many people never take the time to answer this question.

And of those who do answer it, a large number have only nebulous dreams and goals. I want you to do more. Today, I want you to create a personal mission statement.

To complete this exercise — which is based on the work of time-management guru Alan Lakein — you'll need about an hour of uninterrupted time. You'll also need a pen, some paper, and some sort of stopwatch.

When you're ready, I want you to do the following:

1. At the top of a blank page, write this question: What are my lifetime goals? For five minutes, list whatever comes to mind. Imagine you don't have to worry about money, now or in the future. What would you do with the rest of your life? Don't filter yourself. Fill the entire page, if you can. When you're finished, spend an additional five minutes reviewing these goals. Make any changes or additions you see fit. Before moving on, note the three goals that seem most important to you.

2. On a new piece of paper, write: How would I like to spend the next five years? Spend five minutes answering this question. Be honest. Don't list what you will do or should do, but what you'd like to do. Suspend judgment. When your time is up, again spend five minutes reviewing and editing your answers. As before, highlight the three goals that most appeal to you.

3. Start a page with the question: How would I live if I knew I'd be dead in six months? Imagine that your doctor says you've contracted a new disease that won't compromise your health now, but which will suddenly strike you dead in exactly six months. There is no cure. How would you spend the time you have left? What would you regret not having done? You know the drill: Take five minutes to brainstorm as many answers as possible, then five minutes to go back through and consider your responses. When you're ready, indicate the three things that matter most to you.

4. At the top of a fourth piece of paper, write: My Most Important Goals. Below that, copy over the goals you marked as most important from answering each of the three questions. (If any answers are similar, combine them into one. For instance, if "write a novel" was one of your top answers to the first question and "writing fiction" was a top answer to the second, you'd merge these into a single goal.)

5. The final step requires a bit of creativity. Label a fifth piece of paper "My Mission". Look through your list of most important goals. Does one stand out from the others? Can you see a common thread that connects some (or all) of the goals? Using your list as a starting point, draft a Mission Statement. Your Mission Statement should be short — but not too short. It might be anywhere from a few words to a few sentences. Take as much time as you need to make this the best, most compelling paragraph you can write.

When you've finished, I want you to set aside your Mission Statement and walk away. Go about the rest of your life for a few days. Don't forget about your mission, but keep it in the back of your mind.

YOUR PERSONAL MISSION STATEMENT

After you've had time to stew on things, sit down and review what you've written. How does your Mission Statement make you feel? Can you improve upon it? You want a vision to give you a sense of purpose that drives you day-in and day-out, through good times and bad. Ideally, your mission will do for you what my friend Paul's did for him. It'll be so amazing, so glowing that you're willing to walk blurry-eyed to work each morning to make the money necessary to reach your goal.

"Your Mission Statement isn't permanent. As your priorities and tastes change, and as new opportunities present themselves, your mission will adapt and grow"

"I want to be the best person I can be, both mentally and physically. I want to sample all that the world has to offer by fostering new relationships, exploring new ideas, and daring to try new things. I want to use my skills and experience to improve the lives of others while also improving my own."

Sound boring? Not to me! I wrote this mission several years ago, and it still guides me today. When I set personal goals, I base them on this mission. When I make decisions about where to live and what to do with my life, I use this mission to guide me. Bottom line: This mission shapes the way I manage my money and my life.

AFTER YOU'VE CREATED A MISSION STATEMENT, YOUR NEXT ASSIGNMENT

— if you're willing to accept it — is to brainstorm a list of Next Actions to support your Mission Statement. What kinds of things can you do to help you achieve this goal or pursue this mission? Write down anything that comes to mind.

When you have your list of Next Actions, pick the three you can do most quickly (these should become your short-term goals) and the three that would have the biggest impact on your life (these should become your long-term goals). Focus on these six goals!

What if you're still having trouble coming up with a mission?

Don't give up. Try a different approach. Head to your public library and borrow one of the following books, each of which has great info about figuring out what to do with your life:

- How to Get Control of Your Time and Life by Alan Lakein
- The Seven Habits of Highly Effective People by Stephen R. Covey
- Wishcraft: How to Get What You Really Want by Barbara Sher
- The Magic of Thinking Big by David Schwartz

CHAPTER THREE
TAP THE POWER OF PROFIT

In order to survive and thrive, you need to earn a profit.

You already know profit is the lifeblood of every business. It's like food and water for the human body. Although proper nutrition isn't the purpose of life, we couldn't exist without it. Food and water give us strength to do the stuff that matters most. So too, profit isn't necessarily the purpose of business — but a company can't survive without it.

Here's a secret: People need profit too.

In personal finance, "profit" is typically called "savings". That's too bad. When people hear about savings, their eyes glaze over and their brains turn to mush. Boring! But if you talk about profit instead, people get jazzed: "Of course, I want to earn a profit! Who wouldn't?"

Profit is easy to calculate. It's net income, the difference between what you earn and what you spend. You can compute your profit with this simple formula:

PROFIT = INCOME - EXPENSES

If you earned $4000 last month and spent $3000, you had a profit of $1000. If you earned $4000 and spent $4500, you had a loss of $500.

There are only two ways a business can boost profits, and there are only two ways you can boost personal profitability:

- Spend less. A business can increase profits by slashing overhead costs: finding new suppliers, renting cheaper office space, laying off employees. You can increase your personal profit by spending less on groceries, cutting cable television, or refinancing your mortgage.

- Earn more. To increase revenue, a business might develop new products or find new ways to market its services. At home, you could make more by working overtime, taking a second job, or selling your motorcycle.

When you earn a profit, you don't have to worry about how you'll pay your bills. Profit lets you chip away at the chains of debt. Profit removes the wall of worry and grants you control of your life. Profit frees you to do work that you want instead of being trapped by a job you hate. When you make a profit, you truly become the boss of your own life.

With even a small surplus, the balance of power shifts in your favor.

THE MOST IMPORTANT NUMBER IN PERSONAL FINANCE

Earlier, I asked you to calculate your net worth, the number that acts like a snapshot of your current wealth. Your net worth is the grand total of years (or decades) of profits and losses.

As the authors of a book I love put it, "Your net worth is what you currently have to show for your lifetime income; the rest is memories and illusions." Ouch!

The greater the gap between your earning and spending, the faster your net worth grows (or shrinks). This may seem obvious, but it's important. Everything you do — clipping coupons, asking for a raise, saving for a retirement — should be done to increase your profit and wealth.

But profit doesn't mean much on its own. Is a $1000 monthly profit good or bad? Well, it depends on your circumstances.

If your income is $2000 per month (or $24,000 per year), a $1000 monthly profit is great. That's a saving rate of 50%. Congratulations!

On the other hand, if your income is $20,000 per month (or $240,000 per year), a $1000 monthly profit gives you a saving rate of 5%. That's average at best.

You see, it's not your total income that determines how wealthy you are and will become. Neither is it your monthly surplus. No, the true measure of progress is your saving rate — how much you save as a percentage of your income.

In business, saving rate is called profit margin. Naturally, we're going to call it profit margin too.

Pull out your personal mission statement. Look at your goals.

Your profit margin directly affects how quickly you'll achieve these aims. A profit margin of 20% will allow you to reach your destination twice as quickly as a profit margin of 10%. And if you can save 40% or 60%, you'll get there even quicker. (We'll talk more about how to create a wealth snowball later in this book.)

COMPUTING YOUR PROFIT MARGIN

To find your current profit margin, you need two other numbers: your monthly income and your monthly expenses. For now, let's look at only last month. (You're free to run the numbers on past months or years, but for this exercise, last month is enough.)

Here's how to find your income and expenses:

• If you're a money geek who already generates a monthly income statement (a.k.a. profit-and-loss statement), just grab your total income and total expenses from the form.

• Many of you track your money in Quicken or through services like Personal Capital or Mint. These too make it easy to find your monthly income and expenses. Some will even compute your profit for you.

• If your finances aren't yet automated, it's not too tough to calculate the numbers by hand. Collect your brokerage, bank, and credit-card statements from last month. Use these to total your income and expenses. (You shouldn't have to do this line by line. Most statements total income and expenses separately in some fashion.)

• What if you don't track your money? Start! If you owned a business, you'd keep books. Well, a money boss keeps books too. It's the only way to spot trends and to measure progress. Pick a tracking method and make tracking part of your weekly financial routine.

Now it's time for a little math. To find your monthly profit, subtract your income from your expenses. (If your income was $3500 and your expenses were $3000, your profit was $500.) To find your profit margin, divide your profit by your income. (Using the previous example, you'd divide $500 by $3500 to get 0.14286— a profit margin of 14.3 %.)

Burn this number onto your brain. We're going to spend the rest of this book looking at ways to make your profit margin grow.

If you want to get fancy, run the numbers again. This time subtract your mortgage and car loan and credit-card payments (and so on) from your expenses before calculating profit and profit margin. See how much profit you'll have once you've paid off your debt? Cool, huh?

CHAPTER FOUR
SAVE BIG

You don't need a high income to achieve Financial Independence. Making more money helps, sure, but if you're diligent about cutting costs, it's possible to reach financial freedom on even an average salary.

We're constantly bombarded by messages that wealthy people enjoy lavish lifestyles filled with luxury. From my experience meeting with dozens of millionaires over the past decade, this kind of lifestyle is the exception not the rule.

Most wealthy people I know are quiet millionaires. They practice stealth wealth. But don't just take my word for it. Let's look at what the experts say.

LIFESTYLES OF THE RICH AND FAMELESS

In The Millionaire Next Door, authors Thomas Stanley and William Danko share what they learned through years of academic research into the habits of America's wealthy. Here's one key takeaway:

"What are three words that profile the affluent? FRUGAL FRUGAL FRUGAL…Being frugal is the cornerstone of wealth-building."

They write that millionaires tend to "play great offense" with money – their incomes are much higher than average – but they also "play great defense".

They're not big spenders. They're thrifty. They opt out of consumer culture, making purchases based on their personal needs and wants rather than status and fashion.

"Few people can sustain profligate spending habits and simultaneously build wealth," wrote the authors.

"Millionaires became millionaires by budgeting and controlling expenses, and they maintain their affluent status the same way."

Study after study shows the same thing. To get and stay rich, you have to manage your lifestyle. You can't out-earn dumb spending.

Great. You get it. To achieve your goals, you've got to cut costs.

But how? There are two schools of thought:

• Most money writers emphasize saving on small stuff. They teach how to clip coupons, conserve electricity, and spend less on entertainment. These small wins are usually quick and easy to achieve.

• A few folks urge readers to pursue "big wins". They argue that the quickest road to wealth is to spend less on big-ticket items like your home and your car. The downside to this approach? Big wins take a lot of work, and opportunities to pursue them are rare.

I believe that a smart money boss does both. The 1% practice thrift on a daily basis and seize every opportunity to slash spending on the big stuff.

FRUGALITY IS AN IMPORTANT PART OF PERSONAL FINANCE

You could save maybe 50 cents a day by drinking a glass of water instead of a can of soda. That doesn't mean much if you only do it once, but over the course of an entire year that single change would increase your personal profit by nearly $200. When taken together, many such small economies make a noticeable difference.

SMALL AMOUNTS DO MATTER.

You won't get rich—slowly or otherwise—by cutting your cable bill or growing your own tomatoes. But when small changes are part of an ongoing campaign of saving and investing, they can bring big changes indeed!

THE MAGIC OF THINKING BIG

While it's important to save money on everyday stuff, it's even more important to watch how much you spend on major purchases. By making smart choices on big-ticket items, a money boss can save thousands of dollars in one blow. If you spend fifty grand less when you buy a house, that's fifty grand you never have to earn.

Housing is the biggest expense for most Americans — and by a wide margin. According to the U.S. Bureau of Labor Statistics' 2014 Consumer Expenditure Survey, the typical American household spends exactly one-third of its income on housing, which includes mortgage (or rent), maintenance, insurance, interest, and utilities.

In an ideal world, you'd slash your housing expense by buying an affordable home in a city with a low cost of living.

While relocating to a cheaper home in a cheaper city would probably provide a huge financial reward, it's not exactly easy. A more practical alternative might be to move within your current city. Sell your home (or move out of your rental) and choose something more affordable.

Think about it: If you're an average American who spends $1483 per month on a place to live, dropping that expense by 10% would save you $150 per housing payment. Drop it by 30% and you'll save more than $5000 per year!

"If you're not yet wealthy but want to be someday, never purchase a home that requires a mortgage that is more than twice your household's annual realized income. Living in less costly areas can enable you to spend less and to invest more of your income. You will pay less for your home and correspondingly less for your property taxes. Your neighbors will be less likely to drive expensive motor vehicles. You will find it easier to keep up, even ahead, of the Joneses and still accumulate wealth." — The Millionaire Next Door

Transportation is our second-largest expense in the U.S. We spend an average of $756 per month (17 percent of the typical budget) to get around, including vehicle payments, gasoline, insurance, and repairs. I know Americans love their automobiles. They're loath to let them go, even in the face of logic. But imagine how much you could save if you could cut your car costs in half!

HOW DO YOU DO THAT?

• Sell your current car. Replace it with a used vehicle, one that's fuel efficient. (Side benefit: An older, used vehicle will cost less to insure!)

- Drive your car only when necessary. When possible, bike or walk to reach your destination. (Side benefit: Increased fitness, which also saves you money!)

- Make use of public transportation. (Side benefit: Time to read!)

When I recommend people change the way they get around, I'm usually met with a wall of resistance. Let me suggest that instead of looking for reasons you can't do this, instead look for ways you can. You'll save buckets of money.

Together, housing and transportation consume half of the average American budget. There are enormous opportunities to save if you choose to economize on these two categories. But you can achieve big wins in other areas too.

The Consumer Expenditure Survey shows that the typical household spent $1,786 on clothing in 2014, $4,290 on health care, $2,728 on entertainment, and $6,758 on food (which doesn't include the $782 that went toward alcohol and tobacco).

THE BOTTOM LINE

Here's the secret to financial freedom; I don't care how much you make -- you spend less than you earn. You don't have to like it. You just have to do it. Because that is the secret.

The best way to spend less is to optimize the big stuff.

I'm not saying you shouldn't make your own laundry detergent or plant a vegetable garden. By all means, do these things! But understand that if all you do is the small stuff, your only hope is to get rich slowly. You can do better.

Pull out your personal mission statement. With that in front of you, brainstorm ways to reduce your spending. No idea is too small. No idea is too big. No idea is too stupid. Do a rapid brain dump of any (and all) actions you could take to cut costs. If all your spending were aligned with your goals and mission, where would the money go?

After you're finished brainstorming, pick three specific ways — large or small — you'll reduce spending starting this week. (Examples: I'll walk to the grocery store. I'll sign up for a library card. I'll finally cancel my landline.) Also pick one "big win" that you will work to achieve in, say, the next two years. Make this a big, hairy audacious goal. (Example: We'll go from a three-car family to a one-car family.)

CHAPTER FIVE
EARN MORE

There's no question that frugality is an important part of personal finance—you can't out earn dumb spending—but trying to get rich by pinching pennies is like trying to win a car race by conserving gas. If you want to reach the finish line fast, you can't be shy with the accelerator!

Today, I want to explore a better way to boost your profits. Let's talk about how you can make more money. Whether you're self-employed or working for somebody else, your income is determined by three factors:

- Your knowledge and skills. If you want to earn more, it pays to learn more.

- Your productivity. Both the quality and the quantity of your work affect how much people are willing to pay you.

- Your ability to sell yourself. To be paid what you're worth, you have to ask for it.

If you want to make more money, you have to become more valuable in the job marketplace—and demonstrate that value for the market to see. Let's look at how to make that happen.

THE MORE YOU LEARN, THE MORE YOU EARN

In the United States, education has a greater impact on work-life earnings than any other demographic factor. Your age, race, gender, and location all influence what you earn, but nothing matters more than what you know. That's great news,

Highest education in household	Average annual household income	Increase over level below
Advanced degree	$123,654	46.1%
Bachelor's degree	$84,628	39.5%
Associate's degree	$60,671	26.7%
Some college	$47,891	19.0%
High school diploma	$40,260	43.6%
No high school diploma	$28,031	---

really, because you have total control over your level of education.

How much does schooling matter? Here are some numbers from the 2014 Consumer Expenditure Survey conducted by the U.S. Bureau of Labor Statistics:

The average college graduate makes twice as much as his friend whose education ended with high school.

Even a two-year degree from a community college helps. The average worker with an associate's degree earns twice the annual income of a high-school dropout and 50% more than somebody with only a high school diploma. Two years of community college typically boosts income by $20,000 per year. (That's almost one million dollars during an average 40-year career!)

Similar research from the Current Population Survey shows that education also affects unemployment rates:

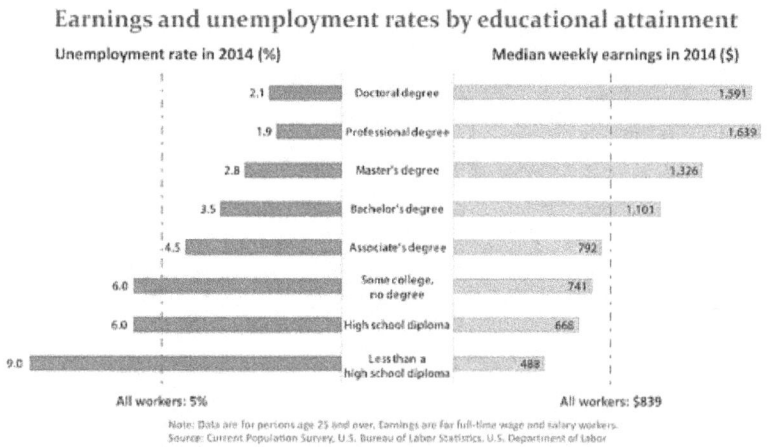

A college degree doesn't guarantee you'll make more money, of course. Some philosophy majors wind up working in convenience stores for the rest of their lives, and some high-school dropouts become billionaires. (Richard Branson is a notable example of the latter.)

If you can't commit to college, it's still possible to improve your knowledge and skills through an ongoing campaign of self-education.

WORK MORE. WORK BETTER.

Education isn't the only factor that affects your income. Your pay is also based on the quality and quantity of your work. If you want to earn more, you can increase the number of hours you work, your output per hour, or the value of your output.

The quickest and easiest way to boost your income is to increase the number of hours you work each week. That might mean going from a part-time employee to a full-time employee. It might mean working overtime. For many folks, it means finding a second job.

Working two jobs can be tough, especially if you have young children. And some people feel like a second job is beneath them. To overcome these objections, recognize that a second job is not a life sentence. It's a way to supercharge your income for the short term.

If you can't add hours to your workday, you can enhance your value by doing more work in the time you have. If you've been producing ten widgets per hours, challenge yourself to produce twelve. If you've been making forty sales calls each week, find a way to do fifty. When you produce more, you're worth more.

In addition to increasing the quantity of your work, it pays to increase the quality of your work. This may seem obvious, but you'd be surprised at how many people "go through the motions" at the office every day. You'll never get ahead if you're only faking it.

It's tough to provide general advice on how to do better work. "Better" varies from job to job. But you know what quality output looks like for your profession. (If you don't, that's a problem you should solve immediately.)

SELL YOURSELF

Your income is dictated by the value of your work, and the value of your work is determined by your education and productivity. But there's one last piece to this puzzle. Your income is also influenced by how well you market yourself.

Like it or not, you are a product. Your work and expertise are commodities.

Your employer wants to pay as little as possible for your work. Your goal, on the other hand, is to be paid what you're worth. To bridge the gap between these two numbers, a smart money boss negotiates his salary.

Think of it like this. When you shop for a new car, you try to pay as little as possible, right? You might need that automobile, but you're not going to pay sticker price if you don't have to. At the same time, the dealer does his best to get you to pay more.

Your boss is the car buyer. She needs an employee but would prefer to pay less than "list price". You're like that car dealership. You want to convince the buyer – your employer – to pay a premium price for your services.

You can increase your lifetime earnings by half a million dollars—or more—if you learn the art of salary negotiation.

It's one thing to know that you should negotiate your salary, but it's something entirely different to do it. What's the trick?

- Delay salary discussions until after you're offered a job. (Same with raises: Discuss a pay increase after your performance review.)

- Let them make the first move. The first person to name a number loses, so always let the employer suggest a salary first.

- When you hear the offer, repeat the top value—then stop talking. This "flinch" is a piece of play-acting that buys you time while putting pressure on the employer.

- Counter the offer with a researched response. Before the interview, do your homework so you know a reasonable salary for the position. Use this knowledge to ask for more. (Start your salary research at sites like Glassdoor and PayScale.)

- Clinch the deal—then deal some more. After you've locked in your salary, negotiate additional benefits like extra vacation days or a company car.

According to a recent study in the Journal of Organizational Behavior, failing to negotiate your starting salary can cost $600,000 during the typical career.

The same ideas apply when asking for a raise. The difference, of course, is that your company already knows whether you're an asset or a liability. To improve the odds of a salary increase during your next performance review, be prepared to state your case. Sell yourself!

Only about half of all employees in the U.S. negotiate their salary.

A money boss always does.

YOU ARE 100% RESPONSIBLE FOR YOUR INCOME

How much you earn directly reflects what the market believes you're worth. Your income is based on the demand for your knowledge and skills, the quality and quantity of your work, and how well you market yourself to potential employers or customers.

"If you want to earn more, you must be worth more"

What the market values might not seem "fair" to you—but "fair" is irrelevant. Is it obscene that professional athletes are paid so much?

Maybe. Should teachers be paid more? Perhaps. But it doesn't matter. These numbers are a product of supply and demand. If you want to increase your income, you have to supply more of what employers want.

Now it's time to act. Spend five minutes thinking about each of these questions:

- What's one thing you can do to increase your knowledge or skillset?

- What's one thing you can do to increase the quantity or quality of the work you do?

- What's one thing you can do to better market yourself to your employer—or to other employers?

For each question, pick one best course of action. Now here's the tough part: Commit to yourself that over the course of the next six months, you'll actually do these three things.

CHAPTER SIX
THINK LIKE A BILLIONAIRE

Whenever you make a choice, there's a cost.

By choosing to buy one item, you pass on the opportunity to purchase other items. By choosing to do one thing, you pass on the opportunity to spend your time on anything else. Opportunity cost is what we give up in order to have the fitting we choose.

LET'S LOOK AT AN EXAMPLE:

Imagine you own a delivery company. You have $10,000 to spend on new equipment. You could buy a new truck to add to the fleet, but then you wouldn't be able to replace the ten-year-old computers in the main office. But if you buy new computers, you won't have as many trucks available to make deliveries. No matter which option you choose, something is lost. That's opportunity cost in action.

While this concept is applied constantly in business, it's often overlooked in personal finance.

When you use money for one thing, that money can't be used for anything else. If you purchase a home with a $1500 monthly mortgage payment, for instance, you can't use that money to travel or to fund your retirement.

Opportunity costs are neither good nor bad. They're simply the price you pay to have what you choose. The problem comes when the choices you make aren't intentional — when you make them out of reflex or habit.

Every time you spend money, there's an opportunity cost associated with it. But you're not just sacrificing other choices in the present; you're also sacrificing your future freedom.

THE MAGIC OF COMPOUNDING

American statesman Benjamin Franklin is credited with having said, "A penny saved is a penny earned." In reality, a penny saved is two pennies earned – or more.

When you buy something, you spend after-tax dollars. If you were to purchase a new $23,000 Mini Cooper, for example, you'd use money left over after paying the government. But in order to get that $23,000, the average American would have to earn $30,000. The other $7000 — in the form of 5-1/2 weeks of work — goes to taxes.

One dollar saved is worth more than one dollar spent.

In the United States, where the tax burden is low compared to other countries, the average worker must earn $1.33 to have $1.00 left over. (In some countries, a worker might have to earn $2.00 to have $1.00 remaining.)

It gets worse!

If you spend one dollar you could have invested, you don't just lose that dollar but any future return you might have earned on it.

Assuming typical stock-market growth, that dollar would have a value of $1.93 ten years from now – and $7.20 in thirty years. (This effect is called "compounding", which Einstein reportedly called "the most powerful force in the universe".)

Now, watch what happens when opportunity cost and compounding come together.

THE WEALTH SNOWBALL

You have to earn more than a buck to have a buck; and if you spend that buck, you're also spending its future value.

On average, each dollar an American spends represents $2.57 of after-tax value in ten years or $9.57 in thirty years. (If you live outside the U.S., the consequences of spending that dollar are probably even greater.)

The bottom line? The opportunity cost of spending one dollar today is ten dollars you could have in retirement.

In fact, this single concept is the cornerstone of billionaire Warren Buffett's vast fortune. He recognized the idea when he was ten years old and it's guided his decisions ever since. Here's a quote from a recent Buffett biography:

"The way that numbers exploded as they grew at a constant rate over time was how a small sum could turn into a fortune. Buffett could picture the numbers compounding as vividly as the way a snowball grew when he rolled it across the lawn. Warren began to think about time in a different way. Compounding married the present to the future. If a dollar today was going to be worth ten some years from now, then in his mind the two were the same."

This idea is so central to Buffett's philosophy that the author named the book after it: The Snowball. (It's a great book, by the way. I recommend it.)

A lot of experts urge people to use the "debt snowball" method to quickly pay down what they owe. I want you to apply the same concept to life after debt.

Your goal, like Warren Buffett, should be to create a wealth snowball.

When you look at things like Warren Buffett, it's easier to see that saving is not sacrifice. When you save, that money's still spent. But it's not spent on a Mercedes or a big house. It's spent buying your future.

The opportunity cost of starting late, a foolish purchase, or a bad investment isn't lost income or lost compounding. It's lost time – lost experience and lost life.

I'm not arguing that you should live like a monk — far from it! — but it's important to consider the opportunity costs of every purchase you make. When you buy something, you should do so intentionally because the opportunity cost of buying on impulse is enormous.

MINDFUL SPENDING

I agree with a concept called conscious spending:

"Being a conscious spender is about making your money match up with your values guilt-free," Sethi says. "It's about spending extravagantly on the things you love while cutting costs on the things you don't." (Some experts use the term mindful spending to refer to the same concept.)

Conscious spending means actively choosing to spend on some things and not on others.

Contrast this with how most people spend.

We buy things because we're expected to. We spend to have what other people have. We sign up for gym memberships that we never use, subscribe to magazines we never read and pay for golf clubs that get buried in the garage. We make impulse purchases at the grocery store – or even on large items, like computers and cars. In other words, we tend to spend without thinking.

The opportunity costs of these unconscious purchases are significant. We're sacrificing our futures for lesser pleasures today.

With conscious spending, you evaluate every purchase, asking yourself:

- "Why am I buying this? Will it make me happier? Will this help me meet my long-term goals?"

- "Would I rather have this now, or would I rather have something bigger and better next year?"

- "Are there other, cheaper options? Could I borrow this? Could I buy it used?"

Mindful spending forces you to become more aware of every purchase you make.

SUMMING UP

In the previous pages, I've shared the nuts and bolts of my financial philosophy. To summarize:

- You are the boss of you. Nobody cares more about your money than you do, so assume responsibility for your financial future. Run your life like a business.

- The best way to get what you want is to become clear on your goals and values. That's why everyone should craft a personal mission statement.

- Profit margin is the most important number in personal finance. Profit gives you the power to do what you want.

- Frugality is the cornerstone of wealth-building, but Big Wins are the best way to spend less.

- You are 100% responsible for your income. To earn more, learn more. Work more and work better. Sell yourself. If you take the time to supercharge your income, your profits will soar.

- Think like a billionaire by carefully guarding each dollar you earn. Recognize that every time you spend today, you're sacrificing a piece of tomorrow. Practice mindful spending.

- Invest wisely. Don't try to get rich quick. Develop an investment philosophy and develop a strategy to back it up.

- Use barriers and pre-commitment to automatically do the right thing – every time.

- As you adopt this philosophy, your wealth snowball will begin to grow. The more you work at it, the bigger it'll get. Protect it. Your wealth snowball is the key to your financial future!

About The Author

Lloyd is a financial advisor and guru who has seen it all. He has a wealth of experience working as a financial consultant working for firms and business owners.

He loves writing books and sharing his wealth of knowledge. His other books include: *Money Management Techniques For The Extremely Rich* and *How To Earn Money In America While Unemployed.*